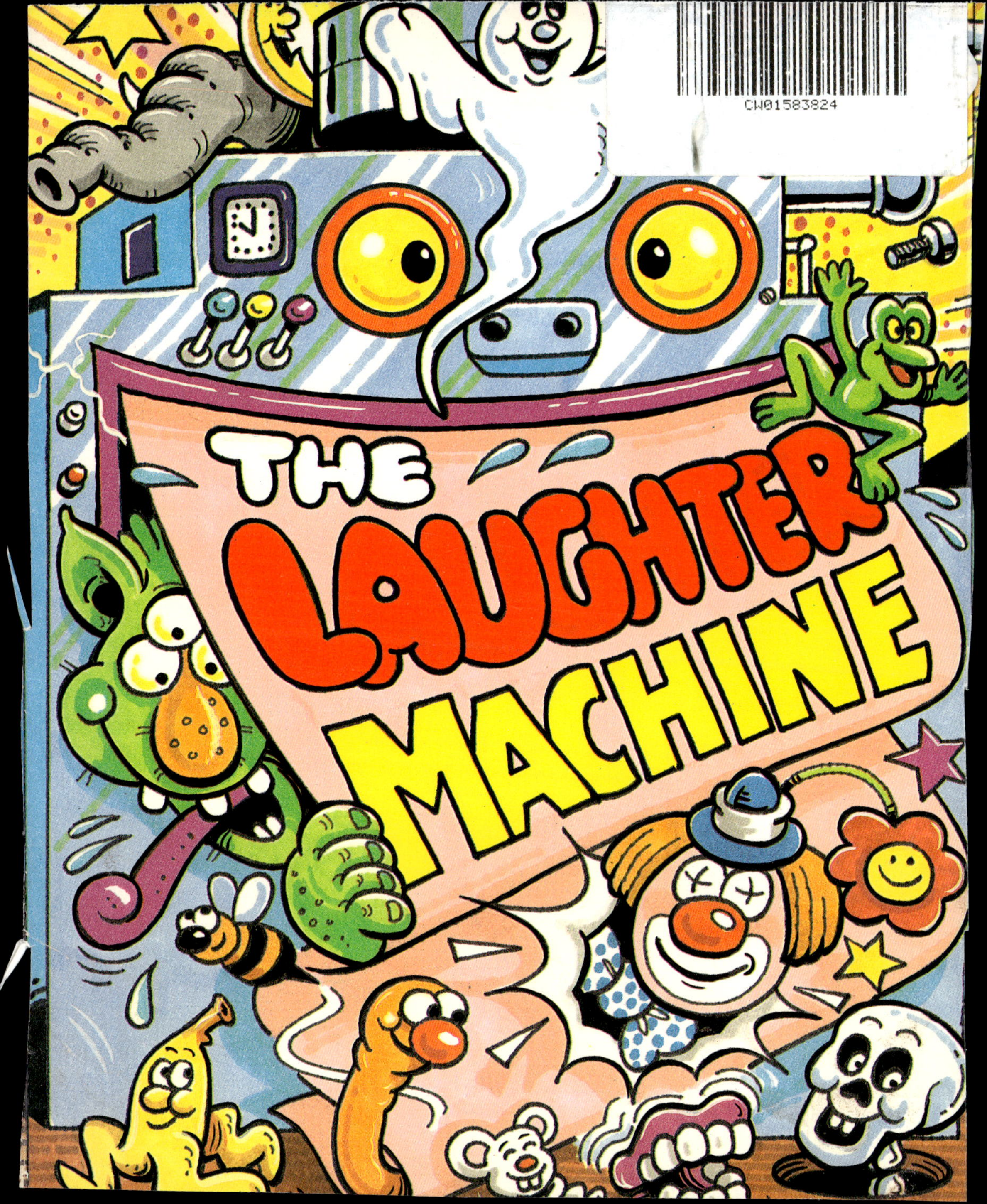
THE
LAUGHTER
MACHINE

WHY ARE ELEPHANTS GREY?
SO YOU CAN TELL THEM APART FROM CANARIES.
MY BROTHER DOES BIRD IMPRESSIONS
REALLY?
YES — HE EATS WORMS
NAME THE FAMOUS INSECT ARTIST?
PABLO BEE CASSO
MUM, AM I POISONOUS?
WHY?
BECAUSE I'VE JUST BITTEN MY LIP.

1. Because they suck seed

2. Grave-y

3. The Barber of Seville

4. A jet setter

5. 'Cos they have two left feet

6. Lord of the Swings

7. It gets hopping mad

8. Harry Elefante

9. Witch-hikers

10. The Red Sparrows

11. Because it has ears

12. A taffy apple

13. 'Dig you'

14. The guillotine

15. Cemetrees

16. A square meal

17. 'Halo there!'

18. Nail varnish

19. John le Curry

20. An exhausted kangaroo

21. A 'nana

22. A pavement

23. Lake Eerie

24. Angel cakes

25. A blazer

26. A young bulldozer

27. Steven Spielbug

28. Vincent Van Cough

29. Truncheon meat sandwiches

30. Shooting stars

31. You're too young to smoke

32. 'Hello, lemon ...'

33. Fox tail soup

34. A snowball

35. F-sssshhhh!

36. A smelly-copter

37. A coat of paint

38. 'Let's split'

39. A mynah bird

40. Put a bucket under it

41. The vampire strikes back

42. Whoa!

43. Henry the ⅛

44. A sunbathing centipede

45. A bloody mary

46. Tish

47. At ghoullege

48. Tea-he-he

1. Why are parrots always clever?

2. What do monsters put on their roast beef?

3. Who shaves the hairs off oranges?

4. What do you call a jelly in a Boeing 747?

5. Why are elephants bad dancers?

6. What book did Tarzan write?

7. What happens to a flea when it gets angry?

8. Who is Tarzan's favourite singer?

9. What do wizards stop for on the motorway?

10. What bird flies fast in formation?

11. Why should you never whisper in front of corn?

12. What's green, sticky and comes from the valleys?

13. What did the archaeologist say to the mummy?

14. What invention gives you a pain in the neck?

15. What trees do monsters like?

16. What does a geometry teacher like to eat?

17. What did the angel say to the other angel?

18. What would you use to polish a screw?

19. What Indian cook writes spy stories?

20. What is 'out of bounds'?

21. Which fruit starts with the letter N?

22. What wears shoes but has no feet?

23. Where do Australian ghosts go on holiday?

24. What does God have for his tea?

25. What jacket is always burning?

26. What do you call a sleeping heifer?

27. Which fly makes films?

28. Which painter always has a bad cold?

29. What do policemen have for their lunch?

30. What kind of stars are dangerous?

31. What did the big fire say to the little fire?

32. What did the orange say to the lemon?

33. What is a fox's favourite meal?

34. Where do snowmen go to dance?

35. What do you call a fish with no eyes?

36. What pongs and flies?

37. What do you put on when its wet?

38. What did one atom say to the other atom?

39. What bird lives down a coal pit?

40. How do you cope with a gas leak?

41. What's Dracula's favourite film?

42. What did Dick Turpin say at the end of his ride?

43. Which king enjoyed doing fractions?

44. What lies on the ground 100 feet in the air?

45. What's a vampire's favourite drink?

46. What do you call a person with a cold?

47. Where do monsters study?

48. What's a witch's favourite drink?

1. A loony module

2. Your word

3. Silicon chips

4. Ee, aw, Marjorie Daw...!

5. Julius Cheeser

6. A frozen silence

7. A laser blade

8. Tyrannosaurus Mex

9. Charles de Ghoul

10. The Milky Bar Kid

11. It kermitted suicide

12. Aston Vanilla

13. The ghoul

14. A seatbelt in a Toyota car

15. Salmon chanted evening

16. A lettuce elite

17. Play squash

18. He lost all his marbles

19. At the Rifle Tower

20. Sherlock Foams

21. A zoo-loo

22. A dead parrot

23. 'Who ghosts there?'

24. Baked beings

25. IV (Ivy)

26. A damson in distress

27. Mittens

28. To the doc

29. Sand-witches

30. In blood banks

31. On April ghoul's day

32. Charles Chickens

33. A kettle

34. A deer hound

35. A female goat

36. It set

37. Huit heures bix

38. It has two banks

39. An eight-sided cat

40. A knicker-bocker gory

41. A U.F.O.

42. Squid-nappers

43. They'd look silly with handbags

44. Tarzipan

45. Burns

46. Khaghouls

47. A match

48. The elves gave him the sack

1. What's mad and goes to the moon?

2. What can you give someone and still keep?

3. What do computers like for tea?

4. What animal is like a nursery rhyme?

5. Which mouse was the emperor of Rome?

6. What's white and deadly quiet?

7. What does Luke Skywalker shave with?

8. Which dinosaurs eat tortillas?

9. Which ghost was a president of France?

10. What do you call a cow with a sheep and a goat?

11. How did the frog die?

12. What do you call a football team with ice-cream?

13. What ghost appears in the play King Lear?

14. What goes 'crunk-crick'?

15. What do fish sing in the South Pacific?

16. What's green and travels at 100 mph?

17. What do elephants do in the back of a mini?

18. Why did the sculptor go mad?

19. Where do Parisians practise shooting?

20. What famous detective liked bubble baths?

21. What's full of animals and quite a relief?

22. What is a polygon?

23. What did the ghost guard say?

24. What do cannibals have for lunch?

25. What Roman numeral can climb a wall?

26. What sits in a bowl and shouts for help?

27. What do you call a cat with a ball of wool?

28. Where does a sick ship go?

29. What do witches like by the sea?

30. Where do vampires keep their savings?

31. When do ghosts play tricks on each other?

32. Who wrote 'Great Eggspectations?

33. What is a water otter?

34. What is the most expensive dog?

35. What's a buttress?

36. Why couldn't the jellyfish swim?

37. What do Frenchmen eat for breakfast?

38. Why is a river rich?

39. What is an octopus?

40. What's a ghost's favourite dessert?

41. What did the astronaut see in the pan?

42. Who snatched the baby octopus?

43. Why do elephants have trunks?

44. What's yellow and leaps from cake to cake?

45. Which Scottish poet is hot stuff?

46. What do ghosts wear on wet days?

47. What's got a brown hat and lies in a box?

48. Why was Father Christmas unemployed?

1. Elf farms

2. The dentist

3. Holes tied together with string

4. Ivan-hoe!

5. The tongue in a shoe

6. Electric-city!

7. They don't know the words

8. A shadow

9. Antibiotics

10. Draughts

11. Somebody using his noodle

12. O positive people

13. I'll never part with you

14. He couldn't stomach him

15. A hippy potamus

16. A magpie

17. A plumpkin

18. Pike Milligan

19. A stuck-up kid

20. Count Drugula

21. North Pole-ish

22. 'Woof woof!' (what else?!)

23. Michsaws

24. Nicholas Nicked-leby

25. He fell off the bonnet

26. Play wom, of course!

27. 'Terror, terror on the wall'

28. A row-bot

29. Cook-oos

30. Buttered host

31. With a witch watch

32. Give me a squeeze

33. A dai version

34. Fission chips!

35. Vitamin bills

36. To rock concerts

37. Mice crispies

38. It was the chickens day off

39. Hard water

40. A four-door banana

41. He went off people

42. 'You little squirt!'

43. Buy it two pairs of stilts

44. They still lie

45. Dates

46. Yvonne Ghoulagong

47. A zebra with a drum-kit

48. He was caught poaching

1. Where do gnomes go to get fit?

2. What does a monster eat after a tooth extraction?

3. What is a net?

4. Who was Russia's greatest gardener?

5. What tongue never speaks?

6. What's the world's most shocking city?

7. Why do bees hum?

8. What can you touch, see but can't hold?

9. What do ants take when they are ill?

10. What's the north wind's favourite game?

11. Who created spaghetti?

12. What type of people do vampires like?

13. What did the bald man say to the comb?

14. Why did the whale let Jonah go?

15. What's heavy and has a flower behind its ear?

16. Which pie can fly?

17. What do you call an overweight pumpkin?

18. Who lives in the sea and tells awful jokes?

19. What do you call a baby goat with a hedgehog?

20. What do you call a vampire junkie?

21. What nationality is Father Christmas?

22. What did the dog say to the cat?

23. What do Irishmen drive in Peking?

24. Which Dickens' character was arrested?

25. Did you hear about the idiot morris dancer?

26. What do you do with a wombat?

27. What does a vampire say to the mirror?

28. What's very intelligent and loves boating?

29. What birds make lunches for people?

30. What do cannibals eat at parties?

31. How does a witch tell the time?

32. What did the toothpaste say to the brush?

33. What do you call a by-pass in Wales?

34. What's the favourite meal of nuclear scientists?

35. What do sick cannibals have for breakfast?

36. Where do geologists go for entertainment?

37. What do cats prefer for breakfast?

38. Why did the duck cross the road?

39. What is ice?

40. What's yellow and goes slam-slam-slam-slam?

41. Why did the cannibal go on a vegetarian diet?

42. What did the big tap say to the small tap?

43. How do you hire a horse?

44. What happens to liars when they die?

45. What fruits do schoolboys hate?

46. Which ghost won Wimbledon?

47. What's black and white and noisy?

48. Why was the cannibal fined £25?

1. A safe robbery

2. Sleep late

3. The milkman

4. The outside

5. The police held an inn-quest

6. In a cowfeteria

7. A chihuahua with a machine gun

8. He had no patients

9. A fence

10. Head first

11. A snake with a lisp

12. The letter G

13. Heavy showers

14. It's a case of bull meets girl

15. A heli-copper

16. In a nest-cafe

17. Pop goes the wee sail

18. Otter mobiles

19. Leap year

20. An elephant on a motorcycle

21. They're both in Seine

22. 'You're having me on'

23. A beef-flat

24. An angel fish

25. A dandelion

26. The hair force

27. Antstronomers

28. A cricket

29. The electric peanut

30. To get some fresh 'air

31. Window-cleaning

32. Birdbrain

33. Stairs

34. Rookside

35. Woolworths

36. Jungle bells, jungle bells

37. Toot-and-come-in

38. From jumping out of trees

39. Ice scream

40. Taurus

41. Something a twain runs on

42. A chocolate-covered elephant

43. Do you believe in people

44. The vampire state building

45. Jaws Formby

46. Your temperature

47. A comb

48. I'm wringing wet

1. What sort of robbery is the easiest?

2. What's the best advice to give to a worm?

3. Where do you get milk from?

4. Which side of a sheep has most wool?

5. What happened when the barman died?

6. Where do cattle eat?

7. What small dog is particularly dangerous?

8. Why was the doctor irritable?

9. What runs but never moves?

10. How do elephants dive into swimming-pools?

11. What's green and slimy and goes hith?

12. What is the end of everything?

13. What are two-tonne raindrops called ?

14. What happens when a cow meets a female?

15. What do you call a flying policeman?

16. Where do birds meet for coffee?

17. What song was sung when the yacht exploded?

18. What animals eat petrol?

19. What's the best year for kangaroos?

20. What's grey, has 2 wheels and weighs 2 tons?

21. Why is a lunatic like a Parisian fish?

22. What did the shoe say to the foot?

23. What key do you sing to a cow?

24. Which fish sits on a cloud and plays the harp?

25. What lion never moves?

26. Which force did the werewolf join?

27. What kind of ants study stars?

28. Which insect loves sport?

29. What did Thomas Edison Elephant invent?

30. Why did the bald man take up jogging?

31. What's the only business you can see through?

32. What do you call an intellectual owl?

33. What goes up and down but never moves?

34. What's a raven's favourite TV programme?

35. What's the favourite store of sheep?

36. What does Tarzan sing at Christmas?

37. How do you use an Egyptian doorbell?

38. Why do elephants have flat feet?

39. What's a ghost's favourite dessert?

40. What's the astrological sign of cows?

41. What's a twack?

42. What's brown, likes peanuts and weighs 2 tons?

43. What did one ghost say to another?

44. What's a vampire's favourite tourist spot?

45. Who menaces the deep and plays the banjo?

46. In hospitals, what's taken but never missed?

47. What's got teeth, but can't bite?

48. What did the bell say when it fell in the water?

1. A puffin

2. An ass mask

3. Slitherpool

4. In his mouth like most people

5. Kung food

6. The bird's eye counter

7. A footballer

8. They both come out at night

9. An unripe elephant

10. A vicious circle

11. The nutcracker

12. Ice burgers

13. Never lend them

14. They like to make a stink!

15. A hentellectual

16. Eight elephants and a giraffe

17. Cygnet-ure tunes

18. D K

19. A swine glut

20. Because seven eight nine

21. Because they're bangers

22. Ghost guard

23. A brick-layer

24. A frog-horn

25. Chocolate moose

26. The scales

27. Net profits

28. Shredded tweet

29. M.T.G.G.

30. Home, home on the range

31. One Scotland Yard

32. A croak and dagger agent

33. Because it's cool Britannia

34. Napoleant

35. Its antchilles heel

36. A shadow

37. A raven maniac

38. Your lap

39. A crazy mixed-up squid

40. True bullievers

41. Monkeys

42. After the bawl is over . . .

43. A leopard with measles

44. 'I've got a crush on you'

45. To sunny Cowlifornia

46. Hold his nose

47. An admiral's hat

48. Tyrantosaurus Rex

1. What bird is always out of breath?

2. What would you wear if you had a mule with BO?

3. What is a snake's favourite football team?

4. How did James Bond like his Martini?

5. What do Japanese wrestlers have for breakfast?

6. Where do sparrows go for treatment?

7. Who gets the most kicks out of his job?

8. Why are false teeth like stars?

9. What's big, green and has a trunk?

10. What's round and bad-tempered?

11. Which ballet do squirrels like?

12. What did the polar bear have for lunch?

13. What's the best system of book-keeping?

14. Why do skunks argue?

15. What do you call a smart chicken?

16. Name nine animals in Africa?

17. What do baby swans dance to?

18. What letters are bad for your teeth?

19. What do you call a pig with a lot of grapes?

20. Why didn't six like seven?

21. Why are sausages so loud?

22. What do ghosts call their navy?

23. What do you call a chicken with cement?

24. What goes croak! croak! when it's misty?

25. What do you call a cocoa bean with an elk?

26. What part of the fish weighs the most?

27. What kind of money do fishermen make?

28. What do you get if a bird flies into a blender?

29. Spell a hungry horse in four letters?

30. What did the cosy kettle sing?

31. What does 36 inches make in Edinburgh?

32. What do you call a frog spy?

33. Why did the Fonz like Britain so much?

34. Who was the famous French ant?

35. What's the weakest part of an ant?

36. What can fall on water without getting wet?

37. What do you call a crazy crow?

38. What gets lost every time you stand up?

39. What do you call a neurotic octopus?

40. What do you call religious cows?

41. What keys are furry?

42. What did the baby's parents say?

43. What's yellow and black with red spots?

44. What did the python say to its victim?

45. Where do cows go for a holiday?

46. How do you keep a skunk from smelling?

47. What's higher than an admiral?

48. What giant ant is now extinct?

1. **Banned Aid**

2. **Pears**

3. **To make both ends meet**

4. **Napolean Baboonaparte**

5. **Joshewea**

6. **A stupid strawberry**

7. **The outside**

8. **Beelicious**

9. **Because it's too far to walk**

10. **Robber ducks**

11. **William the Cornqueror**

12. **A moose**

13. **A clothes horse**

14. **The bell of the ball**

15. **A yak — it's always yakking!**

16. **The Cider Sea**

17. **Before U or I were born**

18. **Tie a knot in your neck**

19. **A bus, it has a conductor**

20. **It has two left feet!**

21. **A comb**

22. **A swimming race**

23. **Blab-boons**

24. **An elephant with measles**

25. **The chief constabull**

26. **Haunting melodies**

27. **A hoptimist**

28. **Polly-filla**

29. **King Kongcord**

30. **To see Gregory Peck**

31. **Pneumatric Krill**

32. **Sore arms**

33. **The hankie-chief**

34. **It had no body to go with**

35. **The hencyclopedia**

36. **The purssian gulf**

37. **A harepiece**

38. **Gnus papers**

39. **Rubees**

40. **Tomorrow**

41. **Who shoves you, baby?**

42. **'You're such a big drip?**

43. **The big cheese**

44. **With a sea saw**

45. **The clock struck first**

46. **A teapot**

47. **Baby-sitars**

48. **Yes sir, it's a butterfly**

1. What's Mrs Whitehouse's favourite charity?

2. Which fruit is never lonely?

3. Why does a dog chase its tail?

4. What ape was the first Emperor of France?

5. What sheep fought at the Battle of Jericho?

6. What's red and grows in an apple tree?

7. Which side of a chicken has most feathers?

8. How do stinging insects taste?

9. Why do birds fly south in winter?

10. What steals soap from the bath?

11. Who is known as the chiropodist king?

12. What animal do you eat for pudding?

13. What horse can't you ride?

14. What rings and dances at the same time?

15. Name the animal that talks the most?

16. What sea makes you drunk?

17. When did the first two vowels appear?

18. How do you stop a cold going to your chest?

19. What transport is safest in a storm?

20. Why's a horse a terrible dancer?

21. What can you give as a parting gift?

22. What race is never run?

23. What kind of apes talk alot?

24. What weighs 2 tons and has red spots?

25. What male is the head of the police?

26. What is a ghosts favourite music?

27. What do you call a cheerful kangaroo?

28. What bird's good for holes?

29. What's big, hairy and flies at 2,000 mph?

30. Why did the star-struck chicken cross the road?

31. What fish do road-menders use?

32. What do you get hanging from trees?

33. Who's the king of the kleenex?

34. Why didn't the chicken go to the disco?

35. What book tells you all about chickens?

36. Where do arab cats come from?

37. What do you give a bald rabbit?

38. What do gnus read in the morning?

39. What's a bees favourite stone?

40. What's always coming but never arrives?

41. What did Kojak say to Ironside?

42. What did the sink say to the tap?

43. What do you call the boss of a dairy?

44. How did Moses part the red sea?

45. Why did the baker hit the clock?

46. What starts with T, ends with T and is full of T?

47. What do they call small Indian guitars?

48. Waiter! Waiter! There's a fly in my soup?

1. A quarter to four
2. Winnie the Pooh
3. A lime bomb
4. A mime bomb
5. A skeleton crew
6. An umbrella
7. 'Do you want a lift?'
8. The other half
9. Attila the Fun
10. They both have to drill
11. Boo-ots and ghoul-oshes
12. The sugar beat
13. A towel
14. Fang mail
15. Get out of the way!
16. A donkey
17. The bat
18. Custard with beri-beri
19. It's too heavy to lift
20. Kick him in the shins
21. When there are four of them . . .
22. A goose-berry on holiday
23. A gold-blooded reptile
24. Heat, you catch a cold
25. Take away its credit
26. Count Duckula
27. Cheer him up
28. Tyranno-saurus Cheques
29. The fang tango
30. From ghost to ghost
31. Phil McCavity
32. Columbus
33. Rheumatism in the hip
34. Petrifried!
35. High stakes
36. To feed her nightmare
37. Elephantom!
38. I'll meet you round the corner
39. They don't want to fall out
40. Oiled lang syne
41. Terry No-gun
42. Peking
43. Neck
44. After a plane trip
45. She fell out of the tree
46. Skint Eastwood
47. On Top of the Cops
48. The Hay Team

1. If 16 boys shared a cake, what is the time?

2. What do you call a bear with a skunk?

3. What's green, bitter and explodes?

4. What's very quiet and explosive?

5. Who man's the ghoul's ship?

6. What goes up but can't go down a drainpipe?

7. What did the jack say to the car?

8. What looks like half a loaf of bread?

9. Which famous comedian sacked Rome?

10. Why are soldiers and dentists similar?

11. What do ghosts wear in the rain?

12. What's the sweetest rhythm?

13. What gets wetter as it dries?

14. What do postmen give to vampires?

15. What do you do if an elephant sneezes?

16. Which key will open no door?

17. What animal is the best cricket player?

18. What's yellow and dangerous?

19. Why can't you put an elephant in a sandwich?

20. How do you make a Maltese cross?

21. When do elephants have sixteen feet?

22. What is green, hairy and wears sunglasses?

23. What do you call a rich dinosaur?

24. What travels faster heat or cold?

25. How do you stop a rhino charging?

26. What has feathers, fangs and goes quack?

27. What do you do with a blue elephant?

28. What do dinosaurs pay bills with?

29. What's a vampire's favourite dance?

30. How do monsters travel?

31. What do you call an Irish dentist?

32. Which bus crossed the ocean in 1492?

33. What is hypnotism?

34. How do ghosts like their eggs?

35. What do vampires play poker for?

36. Why did the woman take hay to bed?

37. What do you call an elephant ghost?

38. What did one wall say to the other wall?

39. Why do birds in a nest always agree?

40. What does JR sing at new year?

41. Which TV star is a karate expert?

42. What capital city cheats at exams?

43. What do romantic vampires do?

44. When would you be glad to be down and out?

45. How did the idiot break her arm raking leaves?

46. What cowboy is always broke?

47. Where would you hear Kojak singing?

48. What group of heroes protects farmers?

1. He was writing sheet music

2. A cuckoo cluck

3. For jogging of course

4. Brake dance

5. Engineers

6. Chop sueycide

7. Coronation Tweet

8. Holy smoke

9. On the tad pole

10. It had a terrible tuskache!

11. The dandy lion

12. They were all in a quiver

13. Supper

14. Woody Woodpickle

15. Some bright spark

16. Attila the Nun

17. To purrgatory

18. Soul music

19. A camel-ion

20. Planet of the grapes

21. Hi! Tiddly Iti

22. 'Bones'

23. To the prawn-broker

24. Tell it to buzz off

25. To tan their hides

26. He counts coppers

27. A glacier mint

28. Yes, no, yes, no, yes . . .

29. Skeleton keys

30. He stole the show

31. Iced lolly

32. Oldham

33. Jaws

34. Wally mixtures

35. By central bleating

36. The royal mint

37. Because it was a moth ball

38. Scotch eggs

39. 'Watts up, doc?

40. Rugbee

41. They may get a hole in one

42. A lunar-tick

43. Intruder window

44. Sting

45. Meow!

46. Pork scratchings

47. Eskimoos

48. Because he liked crumby jokes

1. Why did Mozart stay in bed all day?

2. What do you call a crazy chicken?

3. Why do elephants wear running shoes?

4. What do cars do at the disco?

5. What kind of ears does a train have?

6. What's chinese and deadly?

7. What's a budgie's favourite soap opera?

8. What would you get if you set fire to a nun?

9. Where do frogs fly their flags?

10. Why did the elephant go to the dentist?

11. What's the smartest animal in Africa?

12. Why did the arrows shake?

13. What can't you have for lunch, breakfast or tea?

14. What's green and pecks at trees?

15. Who invented fire?

16. Which holy woman attacked Rome?

17. Where do cats go when they die?

18. What do angels dance to?

19. What's got two humps and changes colour?

20. What's purple and flies in outer space?

21. What do you call a drunken Italian?

22. What would you call a skeleton doctor?

23. Where do fish go to borrow money?

24. How do you make a banana split?

25. Why do cows go to sunny beaches?

26. What does a cashier in a police station do?

27. What's huge, icy and tastes delicious?

28. Are my indicators working?

29. What do bony people use to open doors?

30. What did the dog do at the flea circus?

31. What do eskimoes call money?

32. Which town makes terrible sandwiches?

33. What barks and kills swimmers?

34. What sweets do idiots like best?

35. How do sheep keep warm in winter?

36. What mint can't be eaten?

37. Why couldn't the butterfly get into the dance?

38. What do you get if you give a chicken whisky?

39. How does an electric rabbit greet you?

40. What's a bee's favourite sport?

41. Why do golfers wear two pairs of trousers?

42. What do you call a clock in space?

43. How did the burglar get into the house?

44. Who's top of the pops in the beehive?

45. What do cats do, that no other animal does?

46. What do you get if you cross a pig with a flea?

47. What kind of cows live in the far north?

48. Why did the boy keep biscuits in his comic?

1. No eye-deer
2. Still no eye-deer
3. Snoopbee
4. He had a very sharp wit
5. A Norwegian motor car
6. A Moscow-ito
7. With loud ape-plause
8. Trunkated
9. Make a noise like a banana
10. A frog sandwich
11. Double Dutch
12. The Pink Panter Show
13. A dual cabbage-way
14. A jet setter
15. Hide all the trowels
16. Birds of prey
17. Wheel-burrows
18. Cat
19. Baah-aahd
20. Drop it a line
21. Cow-lypso music
22. Portu-geese
23. 'Oil be seeing you'
24. The Sioux
25. Mice cubes
26. A leek
27. For some foul purpose
28. A false alarm clock
29. Flash Gordon
30. Paddy long legs
31. The Mississippi
32. Drink it when it's fresh
33. Yes, they're very stable
34. A seasick pig
35. A grape is red
36. Stars and spikes forever
37. 'Must fly now'
38. He'd lost his bat, man
39. He fell into a pot of honey!
40. Magpies
41. A hamburglar
42. An ape-ron!
43. Takeway kung food
44. The baa-haa-mass
45. A J
46. A strawberry in a lift
47. Gossip!
48. Tongue salad

1. What do you call a blind deer?

2. What do you call a blind deer with no legs?

3. Name the favourite cartoon character of bees?

4. Why was Mac the Knife so amusing?

5. What is a fjord?

6. What do you call a flea that lives in Russia?

7. How do gorillas show they like a performer?

8. What do you call a 1 metre high elephant?

9. How do you attract a monkey in the jungle?

10. What's white outside, green inside and hops?

11. What language do twins speak in Holland?

12. What's the most breathless thing on TV?

13. What are two rows of cabbages called?

14. What do you call a dog with concorde?

15. How do you stop moles digging in the garden?

16. What birds spend all their time on their knees?

17. What do rabbits call mobile homes?

18. Spell mousetrap using only three letters?

19. How does a sick sheep feel?

20. How would you send a message to a shark?

21. What music do bulls like best?

22. What kind of birds are found in Portugal?

23. What did the pipeline say to the drill?

24. Which Red Indian tribe has the most lawyers?

25. What do you get if you put Jerry in the freezer?

26. What vegetable needs a plumber?

27. Why did the dirty chicken cross the road?

28. What kind of alarm clock never goes off?

29. Who was the showiest cartoon character?

30. What did Wally call the Irish mayfly?

31. What has four eyes but cannot see?

32. What's the best way to stop milk going sour?

33. Are horses sensible animals?

34. What's green and wobbly?

35. How can you tell an ape from a grape?

36. What's a punk's national anthem?

37. What did the pilot say when he took off?

38. Why couldn't Robin play cricket?

39. How did the boy get into a sticky situation?

40. Which pies can fly?

41. What do you call a pig thief?

42. What does a female gorilla wear in the kitchen?

43. What's sweet, sour, dangerous and travels?

44. Where do sheep go for their holidays?

45. What letter is a bird?

46. What's red and goes up and down?

47. What spreads more easily than jam?

48. What kind of salad speaks for itself?

1. It looks round
2. They're both dense
3. To make a hog of itself
4. Milk – when it turns sour
5. A tooth pickle
6. O'rangutangs!
7. Prickled onions
8. To somebody else
9. The feather forecast
10. Cough stirrup
11. Marighouls and mourning-gorys
12. Jelly Savalas
13. Walls of Jericho
14. Peking Toms
15. Hiss fingers
16. John Treevaulter
17. Boy Jaws
18. At parking meteors
19. An old banger
20. No, it hasn't been made yet
21. Birds of prey
22. Holding a pig together
23. Garden hose
24. With cowculators
25. It's boring
26. A tap on the head
27. They quack up
28. He went on a steeple diet
29. Mineopoly
30. The Slave the Childrens Fund
31. With a T-ape measure
32. A milk float
33. An umbrella
34. Moonbeams
35. They get toad away
36. The crane
37. A coconut with a cold
38. When it's henbarrassed
39. At the polytechnic
40. The parrots ate 'em all (paracetomol!)
41. In the river bank
42. Because it's all the rage
43. He had ape-pendicitis
44. A milk sheik
45. So she could hatch-et
46. Ready, set, glow!
47. Gluey Armstrong
48. He melts

1. What does a ball do when it stops rolling?

2. Why is a stupid boy like the Amazon jungle?

3. Why does a pig eat so much?

4. What turns without moving?

5. What's green, sour and cleans teeth?

6. Which monkeys are Irish?

7. What's a hedgehog's favourite meal?

8. What is the best way to serve leftovers?

9. What do geese watch on TV?

10. What do you give a horse with a sore throat?

11. What flowers do ghosts like growing?

12. What's red and wobbles in the sky?

13. What's cold, Israeli and sells ice cream?

14. What do you call Chinese spies?

15. What is a viper's favourite food?

16. What film star jumps over trees?

17. What would you call a young shark that sings?

18. Where do spacemen park their spacecraft?

19. What car is like a sausage?

20. Shall I tell you the joke about the bed?

21. Which birds are religious?

22. What is pigskin for?

23. What do lady strawberries wear for tights?

24. How do farmers count their cows?

25. Heard the one about the woodpecker?

26. What's the cure for water on the knee?

27. What happens when ducks fly upside down?

28. How did the vicar lose weight?

29. What do miners play in the pit?

30. What's Captain Hook's favourite charity?

31. How do you measure the height of a gorilla?

32. What swims and gives milk?

33. What is most useful when it's used up?

34. What holds the moon up?

35. What happens to illegally parked frogs?

36. Which bird can lift the heaviest weights?

37. What's hairy and coughs?

38. When does a chicken get all red?

39. Where do parrots learn to talk?

40. Why are there no aspirins in the jungle?

41. Where do fish keep their savings?

42. Why is it trendy to lose your temper?

43. Why was the gorilla rushed to the hospital?

44. What do you get if you cross a cow with an arab?

45. Why did the chicken sit on the axe?

46. How do you start a race of fireflies?

47. What's sticky and played the trumpet?

48. What happens when a snowman eats a curry?

1. In the Dead Sea

2. Haunting melodies

3. Swamp Lake

4. A monster's bottom

5. Terror-fried

6. His celery

7. Bath

8. Because he had no guts

9. Boys and ghouls

10. 'Hello, Honey'

11. Keep it waiting for two hours

12. Prickly pears!

13. When it turns into a road

14. A toad in der dose

15. Fir

16. A comb

17. A sheep falling off a cliff

18. A polo bear

19. A female moth

20. Spelling

21. Gets wet

22. An invent-tree

23. Because it isn't right

24. Miami Mice

25. Spot

26. A horse

27. An electric elephant

28. A large cheese sandwich

29. Czech books

30. A sunburnt puffin

31. A dead one

32. The Princess of Whales

33. Tyranno-saurus checks

34. He wanted to play squash

35. A divorce-he

36. A dead bus

37. Hose-pipes

38. Because they know all the short cuts

39. Tarzan's coalman

40. The infantry

41. Oilicks

42. He likes to bully-off

43. Give it a spring-clean

44. It has hares in it

45. A pile

46. To oven

47. A jelly fish

48. About one mile an hour

1. Where do ghosts go swimming?

2. What is a ghost's favourite music?

3. Which is the monster's favourite ballet?

4. What's big, green and smells?

5. How do monsters like their eggs?

6. What do you call a vegetable's wages?

7. Where do cleaners live?

8. Why wouldn't the skeleton jump over the cliff?

9. What do you call ghost children?

10. What did the bee say to the flower?

11. How do you make an elephant stew?

12. What fruit do hedgehogs eat?

13. When is a car not a car?

14. What's worse than a frog in the throat?

15. What tree is like a coat?

16. What has many teeth but can't eat?

17. What's white and goes 'baa-baa-splat'?

18. What's furry and minty?

19. What is a myth?

20. What are baby witches good at in school?

21. What does an elephant do when it rains?

22. What do you call a tree that makes things?

23. Why is 4 + 4 = 9 like your left foot?

24. What squeaks as it solves crimes?

25. What did the idiot call his pet zebra?

26. Which animal goes to sleep with shoes on?

27. What's grey and wrinkled and lights up?

28. What is the Cheddar Gorge?

29. What do the citizens of Prague like reading?

30. What's black and white and red at the top?

31. What kind of fish can't swim?

32. What's skinny, well dressed and rules the sea?

33. What tartan do dinosaurs wear?

34. Why did the elephant sit on the tomato?

35. What do you call a man who's wife left him?

36. What's red, has wheels and lies on its back?

37. What pipes are never played in Scotland?

38. Why are hairdressers fast drivers?

39. What's black and swings through trees?

40. Which branch of the army do babies join?

41. What is JR's favourite nightcap?

42. Why does JR play hockey?

43. How do you service a pogo stick?

44. How can you recognize a rabbit stew?

45. What did the inventor of carpets make?

46. Where do all good turkeys go when they die?

47. What lies at the bottom of the sea and wobbles?

48. What was the tortoise doing on the motorway?

1. Roses' Slime juice

2. Jelly beens

3. In the ark'ives

4. Mass hysteria

5. Beethoven

6. A partition made by brickies!

7. Because it was tyred

8. Santaplause

9. A morse toad

10. It's always a wireless

11. Watching telly

12. Stand on his toe

13. A female goat

14. A whino

15. Pussini

16. Lemonade

17. By norse code

18. A chip monk!

19. The Houses of Peppermint

20. He was always snapping

21. Beegonias

22. A flying elephant!

23. They're cream-ated

24. A palm tree

25. Policeman's false teeth

26. At a beastro

27. A soup opera

28. Gooseberry

29. Anywhere it wants to

30. 'Spear me'

31. An ice lolly

32. A mumbo jumbo

33. A gooseberry

34. Quickly

35. Haydn seek

36. A bookworm

37. The jellycatessen

38. He was trying to save time

39. O'levels

40. Because he was skint

41. Bully the Kid

42. Milk of Amnesia

44. Just stable thinking

45. Croakettes

46. They both make a car go

47. Shylock Holmes

48. Hurry up, deers

1. What's a slugs favourite drink?

2. Name the kind of sweets that bees just love?

3. Where did Noah keep the bees?

4. Why did the priest giggle?

5. What composer do bees prefer to listen to?

6. What is a wally?

7. Why couldn't the bicycle stand up?

8. What man claps at Christmas?

9. What's green and goes dit da dit?

10. Why is a radio never complete?

11. What is Kojak's hobby?

12. How do you make a Maltese Cross?

13. What is a buttress?

14. What do you call a dog that drinks too much?

15. Name the famous cat composer?

16. What do you give a hurt lemon?

17. How did the vikings send secret messages?

18. What ape fries potatoes in the zoo?

19. Where do they make laws with holes in them?

20. Why did the boy call his dog camera?

21. Which flower do bees like to plant?

22. What looks like an elephant and flies?

23. What happens to cows when they die?

24. What tree can a gorilla hold in its hand?

25. What's the definition of copper plates?

26. Where do jungle animals eat?

27. What food sings?

28. What do spoil-sport fruits play?

29. Where does a 3 tonne canary sleep?

30. What did the beef say to the kebab skewer?

31. What do you call a freezer with a bank?

32. What is big, grey and mutters?

33. What do you call a gander with a bramble?

34. How should you dress on a cold day?

35. What's a composer's favourite game?

36. What do you call a library with a maggot?

37. Where would you go to buy jellies?

38. Why did the wally put his watch in the bank?

39. What exams do Irish schoolboys sit?

40. Why couldn't the skeleton pay his bus fare?

41. What other bovine is a famous outlaw?

42. What do you get from forgetful cows?

43. What's a blooming nuisance?

44. What is horse sense?

45. What do frogs order for lunch?

46. Why are the goods in a ship like petrol?

47. What detective was a miser?

48. What did the stag say to his children?

1. A nude piano

2. A coat of arms

3. A banana in a washing machine

4. A piano-tuna

5. A sourpuss

6. The toast office tower

7. A lyre bird

8. Hello, sucker!

9. To keep each udder dry

10. Take a coffin break

11. VAT 69

12. Scotch-eggs

13. They've only got one boot

14. A nun on roller skates

15. Air ghostess

16. Shirley Bassett

17. Pat

18. Because they're crackers

19. Pen and oink

20. They're afraid of ducks

21. A Chopin list

22. Waspberry jam

23. He just barged in

24. Boiling water

25. They exorcise regularly

26. So they won't go rusty

27. A cashoo!

28. The Bleach Boys

29. Freddie Mercury

30. A badger with nappy rash

31. On his forehead

32. Because he crew so

33. Mick Jaguar

34. To show he wasn't chicken

35. A monster never remembers

36. Holding cows together

37. 'It's Christmas Eve!'

38. Hide all their chairs!

39. An Eskimoo

40. Multipliers

41. Moby Duck

42. At a 'T' junction!

43. Hag-time

44. A Jack Brussell

45. A killer butterfly!

46. A wine-oceros!

47. 'I'm really stuck on you'

48. Ghouldilocks

1. What is the definition of a harp?

2. What does an octopus wear when it's cold?

3. What's yellow and goes round and round?

4. What is a musical fish?

5. What do you call a cat that eats lemons?

6. What has 600 feet and pops up for breakfast?

7. Which kind of bird never tells the truth?

8. What did the lollipop say to the boy?

9. Why do cows lie down when it's raining?

10. What do monsters do each day at 11 o'clock?

11. What is the Pope's telephone number?

12. What did the drunken chicken lay?

13. Why can't cars play football?

14. What is black and white and has eight wheels?

15. Which job did the ghost have on the jumbo jet?

16. Which female singer sings all sorts of songs?

17. What do you call Postman Pat when he retires?

18. Why do idiots eat biscuits?

19. What does a pig use to write letters with?

20. Why are batsmen cowards?

21. What should you take to a music shop?

22. What do you get from wasps?

23. How did Anth-ony meet Cleopat-ra on the Nile?

24. Which water won't freeze?

25. How does a ghost hunter keep fit?

26. Why are goldfish gold?

27. Which nut sounds like a sneeze?

28. Which pop group kills household germs?

29. Which singer sends the Queen's temperature up?

30. What's black and white and red at the bottom?

31. Where was King Solomon's temple?

32. Why did the farmer call his rooster Robinson?

33. Which Rolling Stone travels around in style?

34. Why did the cockerel cross the road?

35. How can you tell a monster from an elephant?

36. What is a cow-hide most used for?

37.What did Adam say on the day before Christmas?

38. How do you make a bandstand?

39. What is an Eskimo's cow called?

40. Which tools do we use in arithmetic?

41. What do you call a whale with a duckling?

42. Where do motorist's get a nice cuppa?

43. What music do witches play on the piano?

44. What do you call a dog with a vegetable?

45. What's pretty, has wings and a machine gun?

46. Which animal do we get wine from?

47. What did the chewing gum say to the shoe?

48. Which monster made friends with three bears?

1. An elephant on a pogo stick

2. He wanted to grow canaries

3. 'B natural'

4. Cannibulls

5. An ewemorist (humourist)

6. John McEn-Rover

7. Jack the Kipper

8. Iron ones would rust

9. Stingapore

10. Lambo

11. Twisting the night away

12. Dick Gherkin

13. Boy Gorge

14. John McEnrude

15. Lulu

16. A ball-point banana

17. Mrs Christmas

18. Half a centipede

19. A woman with only one child

20. Tomb it may concern

21. Stay in the living room

22. Olive Oil

23. It's way above your head

24. At a jungle sale

25. 'Cos they're groan ups

26. Not safaris I know

27. Lyons quick brew

28. Queen's Pork Rangers

29. Ho-Ho-Hovis!

30. Tee-time

31. Ready neck

32. Incorrectly

33. Hare mail

34. When it's a ruler

35. He was a watch dog

36. Moo-sical chairs

37. Napoleon Boneypart

38. Gungha Din

39. Windscreen Vipers

40. A disco for cakes

41. Very carefully

42. Pine a lot

43. Because it's always in bed

44. Big storks

45. His crypt writer

46. A dumbo jet

47. Because of their amazing feats

48. Mrs Shakespeare

1. What has big ears and hops?

2. Why did the wally plant bird seed?

3. What is the keynote of good manners?

4. What kind of cows eat other cows?

5. What female sheep tells jokes?

6. What's got four legs, barks and plays tennis?

7. What fish terrorizes other fish?

8. Why do elephants have ivory tusks?

9. Where do wasps come from?

10. What do you call a sheep with a machine gun?

11. How does JR spend his evenings?

12. What's green and holds up stagecoaches?

13. What do you call a lad who won't stop eating?

14. Which tennis player makes a bad impression?

15. Which pop star has two toilets?

16. What is yellow and goes click-click?

17. What is Father Christmas's wife called?

18. What has fifty legs and cannot walk?

19. What is the definition of a minimum?

20. How does a ghoul start a letter?

21. How do you keep from dying?

22. Who is JR's favourite cartoon character?

23. Did you hear the joke about the roof?

24. Where does Tarzan buy his clothes?

25. Why are adults boring?

26. Do sailors go on safaris?

27. What drink do jungle big cats prefer?

28. What's pink, has four legs and plays football?

29. What's the happiest loaf in the world?

30. When's the best time to play golf?

31. What does Dracula have for breakfast?

32. Which word is always spelt incorrectly?

33. How do you post a rabbit?

34. When is a piece of wood like a Queen?

35. Why did the dog run in circles?

36. Which games do cows like playing?

37. Who was the thinnest emperor?

38. Name the noisiest hero of all time?

39. Which snakes are used to clean windscreens?

40. What is abundance?

41. How do hedgehogs play leapfrog?

42. What do sad pine trees do?

43. Why is the letter 'E' lazy?

44. What brings baby elephants?

45. Where does Dracula get his jokes from?

46. What do you call an elephant that flies?

47. Why do heroes wear big shoes?

48. Who was the first Avon lady?

1. Well, I'll be doggone

2. Give him a hand

3. The Ghosta Brava

4. They always go up in the world

5. O.I.C.U.

6. Jan Lemming

7. With a victim cleaner

8. He had a screw loose

9. A 2 year old calf

10. Chase it round the garden

11. Draw!

12. A methylated spirit

13. Bridesmaids

14. Hatch of the day

15. Little donkeys

16. The dark

17. 'The Ghoul on the Hill'

18. Rustling

19. When you're in it

20. To keep your leggies up

21. They loved in vein

22. Very crude oil . . .

23. Chirrup of figs

24. A ghoulage

25. When the rain's dripping

26. In a moo-seum

27. It has a tender behind

28. A drip-dry grapefruit

29. A migloo

30. A recipe spook

31. Bug Rogers

32. Bald Automatic

33. 'What kind of fuel am I?'

34. 'You big drip!'

35. Septic parrots

36. A tree

37. Wet, sweetie

38. Ghouldi-locks

39. A tap dance

40. Its bark

41. It has too many locks

42. An E-type jab

43. Say 'giddy-up!'

44. A zeedonk

45. A hot dog!

46. A big dripper

47. In Hyde Park

48. An astronut

1. What did the dying dog say?

2. What should you do for a starving cannibal?

3. Where do ghosts go on holiday?

4. Why are astronauts such successful people?

5. What letters would frighten a burglar?

6. Which news-reader jumps off cliffs?

7. How does a vampire clean his house?

8. Why was the space robot so silly?

9. What is a calf after it is 1 year old?

10. How do you make puffed wheat?

11. What did the cowboy say to the artist?

12. What do you call a drunken ghost?

13. Who holds up trains but are never arrested?

14. What's a hen's favourite TV programme?

15. What are assets?

16. What does a cat turn into when the lights go out?

17. What's a ghost's favourite Beatles' song?

18. What did the paper cowboy get arrested for?

19. When do you go as fast as a space rocket?

20. What are hippies for?

21. Did you hear about the two blood cells?

22. What comes from the desert and shouts 'bum!'?

23. What do you call a constipated budgie?

24. What's a ghost's favourite work of art?

25. When are pavements most slippery?

26. Where would you find a prehistoric cow?

27. Why can't a steam engine sit down?

28. What's yellow and never needs ironing?

29. What's made of ice and shoots down spitfires?

30. What ghost is handy in the kitchen?

31. What do you call an insect from outer space?

32. What is Kojak's favourite washing powder?

33. What did the coke say to the coal?

34. What did the small tap say to the big tap?

35. What's green and sings in cages?

36. What has 100 limbs but cannot walk?

37. What does Father Christmas call reindeer?

38. Which ghost ate too much porridge?

39. What dance do you do in the bathroom?

40. What makes a tree noisy?

41. Why hasn't anyone stolen the Thames?

42. What's fast and pricks?

43. How do you shoe a horse?

44. What do you call a zebra with a donkey?

45. What breed of dog has no tail?

46. What's wet and makes you scream?

47. Where did Dr Jekyll find his best friend?

48. What do you call a crazy spaceman?